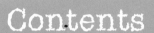

Contents

Written by Dr Andrew Ross

What are fossils?

Fossils are the **remains** of animals and plants that lived millions of years ago. You may find the fossilised shell or bones of an animal that's been **preserved**, or the shape of an animal or plant that rotted away. You can also see marks, like footprints, left by animals. These are called trace fossils.

dinosaur skull fossil

Sometimes you may find insects trapped in amber – a liquid from trees that has gone hard over time.

clam fossil

insect in amber

2

People who study fossils are called palaeontologists.

When they discover a fossil, they try to find out all about it.

They write down where it was found and what rock it was in.

Once they know what kind of fossil it is, it's stored in a museum.

How are fossils made?

An animal such as a dinosaur dies. Its soft insides get eaten by other animals.

Its bones are quickly covered with thick layers of mud.

Over a long time the mud gets squashed and it hardens into rock. The bones are preserved in the rock.

Millions of years later someone finds the fossil dinosaur bones in the rock.

Where can you find fossils?

Fossils are found all over the world. If you'd like to go fossil hunting, the seaside is a good place to look. Waves crash against the cliffs and wash bits of rock away, showing the fossils hidden inside.

6

How old are fossils?

Palaeontologists can tell how old fossils are by looking at the rock where they found them. Some fossils are more than 500 million years old. The timeline shows when some different fossil animals and plants lived.

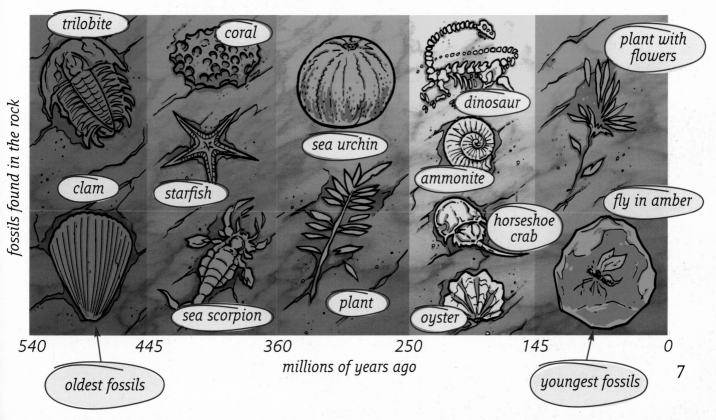

fossils found in the rock

trilobite

coral

plant with flowers

dinosaur

sea urchin

ammonite

clam

starfish

fly in amber

horseshoe crab

sea scorpion

plant

oyster

540   445   360   250   145   0

millions of years ago

oldest fossils

youngest fossils

7

Ammonites

If you're at the seaside, a common fossil you may find is a sea creature called an ammonite. Look carefully for spiral shapes in the rock – the ammonite looks like a curly ram's horn. If you're lucky enough to find one, you'll be holding a fossil that is more than 65 million years old. Ammonites are now **extinct**.

Ammonites swam backwards and had tentacles to catch food.

fossilised shell of an ammonite

coiled (spiral) shell

A sharp beak and tentacles would have been here.

ribs

9

Corals

You can also find fossilised coral at the seaside. Corals look like plants, but they're actually lots of little animals that live together. They grow in warm, shallow seas and form big **reefs**. Some coral fossils are more than 400 million years old. When you're hunting for coral fossils, look out for different shapes.

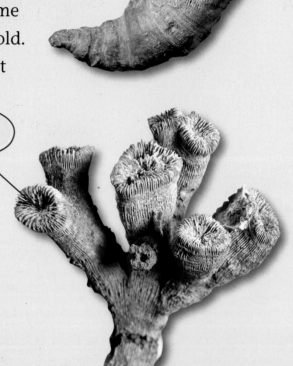

horn-shaped coral fossil

branching-shaped coral fossil

dome-shaped coral fossil

Coral fossils have been found all over the world. Today, the largest living coral reef is in Australia. It's so big you can see it from space.

the Great Barrier Reef, Australia

You can see the branching and dome shapes, just like the fossils.

11

Clams and oysters

Fossilised **clams** and **oysters** look just like the live ones you can find at the beach today. You may find them with their two shells joined together, or just one shell if it has fallen apart.

You can see both halves of this clam shell fossil.

Curved ribs on this oyster fossil make the shell stronger.

living clams

12

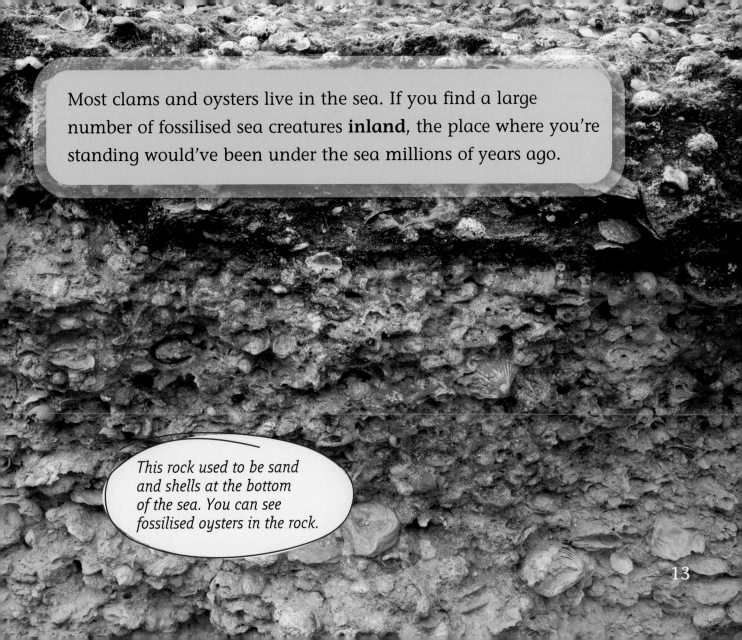

Most clams and oysters live in the sea. If you find a large number of fossilised sea creatures **inland**, the place where you're standing would've been under the sea millions of years ago.

This rock used to be sand and shells at the bottom of the sea. You can see fossilised oysters in the rock.

13

Sea scorpions and crabs

Sea scorpions have legs with **joints** (like the legs of a spider or a crab). Millions of years ago sea scorpions were much bigger than scorpions you can see on land today. The largest sea scorpion was 2.5 metres long, so when you go fossil hunting, what you find may only be a little bit of something much larger.

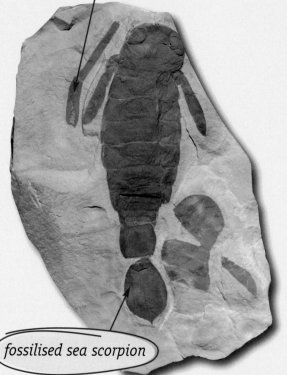

Some sea scorpions had long, sharp pincers to grab fish.

fossilised sea scorpion

This is what sea scorpions would have looked like when they were alive.

Some creatures, like horseshoe crabs, look the same today as they did millions of years ago. These animals are called living fossils.

fossilised horseshoe crab

a horseshoe crab that you may find on a beach in America

15

Trilobites

Some sea creatures lived together in large numbers. If you find a fossil of a **trilobite**, look hard – there may be more.

living trilobites

Trilobites are now extinct. These are trilobite fossils.

There were lots of different kinds of trilobites, so look out for the different shapes.

Some had smooth heads … while others were knobbly.

Some had rounded tails … and others had triangular tails.

Sea urchins and starfish

Some sea urchin fossils are heart-shaped, others are round.

Look out for sea urchins and starfish in rock pools at the seaside. Sea urchins have a round shell covered in spines that protect them from being eaten. But if you find a fossilised sea urchin, you'll usually only be able to see its body because the spines fall off after it dies. Sometimes you find the fossil spines nearby.

living sea urchins

18

Starfish fossils are hard to find, because they're **fragile** and break easily. You'll know if you've found one by its shape. It usually has five arms and looks like a star, just like the ones alive today. Some starfish have longer arms than others. These arms help the starfish to crawl around on the seabed, or climb rocks to find food.

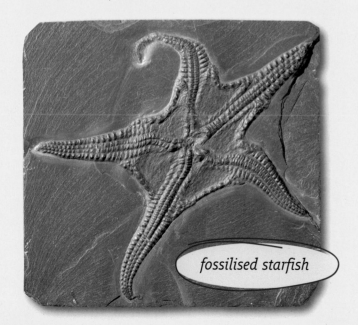

fossilised starfish

living starfish

Plants

Not all fossils were animals. There are many different kinds of plant fossils, which have been preserved in mud. You may see fossilised leaves, branches or fir cones.

This fossilised leaf looks the same as leaves you can see on ferns today.

Even fossilised **pollen** has been found, but you need a powerful **microscope** to see it.

fossilised pollen

The first plants on land appeared more than 400 million years ago, but these were small, like moss. Over time this changed, and 300 million years ago some ferns grew as big as trees.

You can also find the shape of bark and branches, where plants have rotted away and left only marks in the rock.

fossilised branch

Trace fossils

Trace fossils are marks that were left by animals when they moved about. They're not the animals themselves, so they're not shells or bones. Different kinds of animals made different tracks or trails as they walked or burrowed through the mud looking for food.

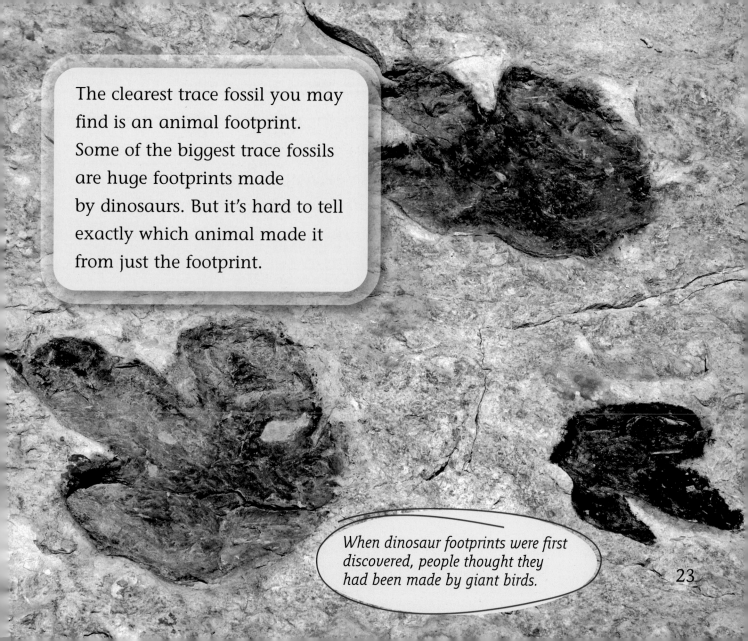

The clearest trace fossil you may find is an animal footprint. Some of the biggest trace fossils are huge footprints made by dinosaurs. But it's hard to tell exactly which animal made it from just the footprint.

When dinosaur footprints were first discovered, people thought they had been made by giant birds.

23

Dinosaurs

Complete dinosaur fossils have been found in North America, South America, China, Mongolia and Africa. Millions of years ago, all these places had lakes, rivers and swamps – ideal for preserving large animals that may have got stuck and drowned.

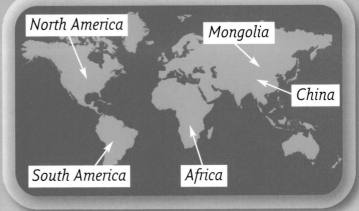

North America

Mongolia

China

South America

Africa

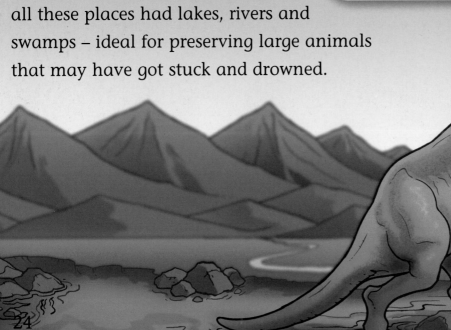

Dinosaurs were the biggest land animals that ever lived. Fossils of dinosaur bones, teeth, footprints and droppings can tell us lots about what they were like. Fossilised teeth can tell us if a dinosaur ate meat or plants.

Even dinosaur droppings can tell us if they ate meat or plants.

This dinosaur ate other animals, so its teeth needed to be sharp and pointed to rip through meat.

25

Often only a single bone of a dinosaur is found and it's hard to tell exactly what animal it is until you've dug up the whole dinosaur.

a palaeontologist uncovering a dinosaur fossil

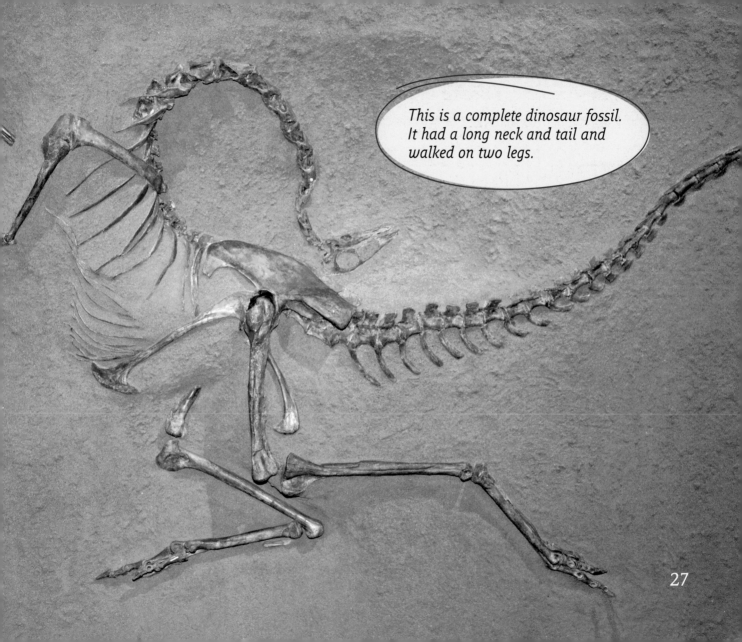

Glossary

clams	creatures that live in water and have two shells of the same size
extinct	a type of animal or plant that no longer exists
fragile	something that is easily broken
inland	land that is not near the coast
joints	where two or more bones meet
microscope	an instrument that makes small objects look much bigger
oysters	creatures that live in water and have rough, uneven shells
pollen	powder made by plants
preserved	something that has been protected and doesn't change over time
reefs	underwater ridges, where the tops are just below the water
remains	what is left after something has died
trilobite	a sea creature that is now extinct

Index

Let's go fossil hunting

clam fossil

ammonite

Fossil hunting kit

your eyes!

goggles

hammer

coral fossil

starfish fossil

dinosaur bones

fern leaf

sea urchin fossil

dinosaur footprints

sea scorpion

trilobite

cold chisel with
a plastic hand guard

safety helmet

magnifying glass

paper to wrap
the fossil in

notepad

Ideas for guided reading

Learning objectives: draw together ideas and information from across a whole text, using simple signposts in the text; explain organisational features of texts, including alphabetical order, layout, diagrams, captions; explain their reactions to texts, commenting on important aspects; explain ideas and processes using imaginative and adventurous vocabulary and non-verbal gestures to support communication

Curriculum links: Geography: Going to the Seaside

Interest words: fossils, remains, fossilised, palaeontologist, trilobite, clam, coral, sea urchin, dinosaur, ammonite, oyster, extinct, tentacles, inland, pincers, trace fossil, preserving

Word count: 1,385

Resources: ICT

Getting started

- Look at the front cover together. Ask children to describe what they can see and what they think it is. Look for the distinct parts of the skeleton fossil.

- Read the blurb with the children. Ask them to describe the ammonite fossil on the back cover in detail.

- Turn to the contents. Explore how the contents are organised, e.g. with the first chapters answering general questions about fossils, and the remaining chapters providing information about different types of fossil.

- Notice the index and glossary sections. Ask children what they can be used for and read the entries and their definitions.

Reading and responding

- Turn to pp2–3. Read these pages to the children. Ask them to follow the words, and to identify any new or tricky words, e.g. preserved. Check that children understand the meaning of new words and remind them of strategies to help them decode the word.

- Ask children to read pp4–5 silently. Challenge them to recount to a partner the four stages that describe how a fossil is made.